100 Days

JULIANE OKOT BITEK

100 DAYS

THE UNIVERSITY OF ALBERTA PRESS

Published by

The University of Alberta Press
Ring House 2
Edmonton, Alberta, Canada T6G 2E1
www.uap.ualberta.ca

Copyright © 2016 Juliane Okot Bitek

LIBRARY AND ARCHIVES CANADA
CATALOGUING IN PUBLICATION

Okot Bitek, Juliane, 1966-, author
    100 days / Juliane Okot Bitek.

Poems.
Issued in print and electronic formats.
ISBN 978-1-77212-121-6 (paperback).—
ISBN 978-1-77212-152-0 (EPUB).—
ISBN 978-1-77212-153-7 (kindle).—
ISBN 978-1-77212-154-4 (PDF)

    1. Genocide—Rwanda—Poetry.
I. Title. II. Title: One hundred days.

PS8553.I87757054 2016   C811'.54
C2015-907547-5
C2015-907548-3

First edition, second printing, 2018.
First printed and bound in Canada by
Blitzprint, Calgary, Alberta.
Copyediting and proofreading
by Peter Midgley.

A volume in the Robert Kroetsch Series.

All rights reserved. No part of this
publication may be produced, stored
in a retrieval system, or transmitted in
any form or by any means (electronic,
mechanical, photocopying, recording, or
otherwise) without prior written consent.
Contact the University of Alberta Press
for further details.

The University of Alberta Press supports
copyright. Copyright fuels creativity,
encourages diverse voices, promotes free
speech, and creates a vibrant culture. Thank
you for buying an authorized edition of
this book and for complying with the
copyright laws by not reproducing,
scanning, or distributing any part of it
in any form without permission. You are
supporting writers and allowing University
of Alberta Press to continue to publish
books for every reader.

The University of Alberta Press gratefully
acknowledges the support received for its
publishing program from the Government
of Canada, the Canada Council for the
Arts, and the Government of Alberta
through the Alberta Media Fund.

For Yolande Mukagasana
A woman who found words and poetry after the genocide.

Contents

Foreword

IN APRIL 2010, Michaëlle Jean, then Governor General
of Canada, visited Kigali, Rwanda during its national week of
mourning. She formally apologized to Rwandans for Canada's
role as part of the international community that had failed to
act soon enough to prevent the 1994 genocide. Canadians were
encouraged to reflect on the lessons learned. The losses preci-
pitating those lessons remain immeasurable, yet through her
poetic practice Juliane Okot Bitek manages to account for what
she calls "a harvest of death." Even in moments blunted by
anguish, her tack is consistently generative.

The poems in *100 Days* pose incisive questions that deepen
our resolve to witness. Striking through official discourse, the
poetry is multiscalar and delicately local in its attentiveness.
The one hundred days recounted here, "should be days to think /
to consider / to see / to witness." With these poems we learn
about the impossibility of persisting, and yet persisting, through
everyday horror. In her writing, Okot Bitek shows how ripening
markets, colonialism, caste and class division, austerity, war and
political turmoil contribute to violence, gendered violence and
to the conditions for genocide the world over.

With a generous familiarity, Okot Bitek engages and trans-
mutes an African and East-African sense of community, aspects
of diaspora, and transitory belonging within North American
systems and experience. Her poetry compels us to do our own
work to account, relate and strengthen. We remain determined
to create and therefore to act. Although the poems specify land
and people closer to her Ugandan homeland, Okot Bitek's insights
resonate in relation to the genocide of Indigenous peoples in
Canada and elsewhere around the world. However at home we
may be in the traditional and ancestral territories of Indigenous
Peoples, this poetic project is aware of ongoing disjuncture. It

questions the rote offerings of an insincere, immaterial and governmental "reconciliation."

I observed this project's initial unfolding in social media over time and was inspired by the quality of the artists' claims and their wise use of those forums. It is heartening to see the project continue in book form. Juliane Okot Bitek's *100 Days* is so much more than commemoration's "crafted affair." As she responds to Yolande Mukagasana, a survivor whose indomitable spirit inspired this collection, and enters into dialogue with artist Wangechi Mutu, she posts and plaits memory, and with care and resilience is able to grasp a new future.

CECILY NICHOLSON
New Westminster, August 2015

100 DAYS

It was the earth that betrayed us first

it was the earth that held onto its beauty
compelling us to return

it was the breezes that were there
& then not there

it was the sun that rose & fell
rose & fell

as if there was nothing different
as if nothing changed

Could relate to
the fact the rest
of the world carried
on and ~~hartley~~
hardly gave aid
and left Rwanda to
fend for themselves

Day 99

It was sunrise every morning
the same land
same sky
same rivers
hills & valleys

it was the same road that led away & back home
the same sweet air that amplified the voices
through whispers   gossip   airwaves

words leapt into our eyes
& burned this new knowledge that was never new

but it was the earth that betrayed us first
in those one hundred days that would never end

no matter what
happened or who
died, the earth
and scenes stayed
the same

Day 98

If this should be a list of betrayals where should we begin

at last we're here

at last we're gone

what is this life beyond one hundred days
what is this life beyond one hundred days

twenty times over
what days are left

we were already *in medias res*
we were always inside one hundred days

even when the
100 days ends.
what happened
still happened +
so much happened in
so little time.

Day 97

The poet told us of her brother
the poet told us of her drunken brother
speaking of his dreams

He was an alcoholic
he was always drunk

the poet told us about her drunken brother
who spoke of his mad mad dream

she told us how he spoke
like a mad man
about this dream

like a prophet insisting on an unknown truth
like the drunken man that he was
imposing a faith that no one wanted to hear
like Jesus
like all the holy prophets
(even the ones we forgot)

the poet told us about her brother
who spoke of a dream in which everybody would die
they would kill everybody

except me she said
except me

What is the essence of beauty
      why do mists swirl & rise
            but never completely disappear
                  why should iron gleam through soil
            why should our dances be graceful
      our clothes bright
memories long
      language rich & layered
            why should beauty render us speechless

what is it to come from a land
that swallows its own people

Day 95

Time   they taught us   was linear & exact
a series of beats
a line extending from the beginning of things

forget that illumination is an indication of knowing
forget that we were trapped inside a hundred days
a hundred days of light
each following the other
each following the other

time bore witness to our erratic heartbeats
but we remain trapped
inside a hundred days
that have morphed
into years
& years

how can we exist outside of betrayal
by time & land

We walked when our legs could carry us
childhood rhythms carried us along
songs from days of innocence
like holding hands
like soft embraces

hinky pinky ponky
hinky pinky ponky
father had a donkey

we needed a rhythm to walk
to move   to drag ourselves along

who could count past four
acel aryo adek aŋwen
who could count past four

hinky pinky ponky
hinky pinky ponky
father had a donkey
donkey die
father cry
hinky pinky ponky

it seemed as though
there was a time before tears

it seemed a dream to think
there was a time when fathers could cry

Day 93

Elsewhere
elections & the winners won
a car chase
the end of one war
the continuation of another

now headlines   now pictures   now memories
now colour   now movement   now silence

nothing reflects the efficiency
with which those days went by

we were betrayed
by a month & a half
that now we call commemoration

We wish for absolution
for a clearing
for a forgetting
a filling of the heart
& joyousness one more time

we wish for children of innocence
we wish for an instantiation of things
& rationality that resonates with our emotions

we wish for the silence of the moon
the quieting of ghosts
& peace to rest in

Day 91

We couldn't have known
nine days in
that it would ever be over

it was a time warp that had us
in flashes & then in woozy moments
that took forever

machete hangs in a museum in Ottawa
a machete hangs perpetually
in a museum
in Ottawa

a machete hangs like a mockery of time
like a semblance of that reality
in which another machete
& other machetes hanged
for what seemed like a long time
but eventually they come down
again & again & again & again & again

even time measured in machete strokes
can never be accurate

How these hundred days
should be days to think
~~about reconciliation & forgiveness~~

to consider ~~the irrationality of ethnic cleansing~~
to see ~~the phoenix rise again~~
~~& grief overcome~~
to witness ~~humanity & good~~
~~& the power of God~~
~~to make miracles~~

ultimately
commemoration is a crafted affair
a beautiful thing
a symbol of power & resonance
in the everlasting flame

to remember
that there is an empty space in our arms
that our lost children will never fill

this is not our liberty
we are not free to forget

Day 89

What do crickets know about innocence
were they not there
did they not see more than we did
by staying closer to the ground than we ever were

innocence in that ghastly cry   why
why do we do this to ourselves

innocence in that other proclamation
never, never, never again

innocence is power without experience
innocence is a knowing untempered

crickets know this
there is no innocence on hallowed ground

Day 88

After all this
time flashes
time drags
nothing as nothing   just as it was
a nothingness

today   a vacuous attempt
to move
to sound
to connect to anyone   anyhow

someday we will grasp
the emptiness
inside one hundred days

Day 87

Reconciliation is a grand thing
reconciliation photographs well
reconciliation makes people smile
reconciliation feels good   dresses well
writes well   conjures good dreams

reconciliation is minding my business
reconciliation is minding my life
reconciliation is aimed at my head
reconciliation leaves me no choice

don't get me wrong

reconciliation wants me to wipe my tears
to wipe the slate clean
it wants me to forget my first born daughter
the one I could not bury

reconciliation
shouldn't erase
or excuse the
past but rather
learn from it &
make amends

My country belongs to God
these are our scriptures

> Happy shall he be
> that taketh and dasheth
> thy little ones against the stones
>   Psalms 137:9

> Vengeance is mine
> saith the Lord
>   Romans 12:19

> I will be there
> where there are two or more
> gathered in my name
>   Matthew 18:20

Jesus must have a permanent presence
in the church where the door
has been propped ajar for eternity

Jesus Christ must live here
where congregants were struck in supplication
pleading for their lives
pleading pleading for their lives

where shall we find comfort
where can we go in this country of God

Day 85

& God said
let there be light
& there was light from the beginning of the world

there was light on this day like all the other days
every day there was light enough to see everything
we didn't always need to see
we didn't need to see everything every day

Impressionistic moments follow each other
like Monet come to life

it's after two in the afternoon
now it's evening
now suddenly night

food   blanket
no food   no blanket
it's all the same

there were no hundred days
just a jumble of impressions
moments that sometimes piled up
on top of each other
moments that sometimes lay side by side
sometimes held hands
or slept hungry
or slept without blankets

Day 83

We failed to read the clouds
as we had been taught to do in high school
cumulonimbus chasing cotton balls
cumulonimbus alone
cumulonimbus with or without rain

what did it all mean
what did it mean that we failed to read the sky
it wasn't in the cowrie-shell readings
it wasn't in the tea

perhaps cumulonimbus was a script in the sky
a kind of writing that was not familiar
not then & definitely not now

Day 82

This is to confirm that there is something to be said
for tying the waist really tight
tight tight tight tight
tighter than when spoiling for a fight
tighter that when getting ready to receive a heavy burden
tight enough for days that rolled upon days

it had to have been the tightness in our waists
that kept us going

Day 81

Nine times
nine times they called out
nine times   just nine

we know this because
each call caused a finger to fall

we know this because
there was one finger left

the ringed one
only the ringed one

There is something inconsequential about all of this
one foot in front of another
one foot in front of another

never again & reconciliation
like wayward birds about my head

a nothing in front of a nothing
round a round
round a round

round a round a round a round a round

blindfold me   or not
here's another spot on the map
where people are walking

one foot over another
one foot over another
for one hundred days

Day 79

A piece of cloth in a breeze
a clump of mud
a memory of desire
a broken yellow pencil with black stripes
Staedtler Noris HB2 Made in Germany
a small stone
a tuft of grass
a faint smell of smoke
a small hill amongst many
a faded sign above the shop reads
oca Cola It's the Real
a child runs across the way

a list of jumbled images
none of which takes me away long enough to forget

From royalty to madness
insouciance has to be blue
from the marked maleness of babies
to those that stayed death
insouciance must be blue

how else to explain a sky that witnesses
& still insists on magical hues of itself

from indigo at midnight
to the peasant hue of the mother of God
another young woman
to whom a hole in the pale blue announced
that she would bear a child
that she would bear
a boy dressed in madness

how else can we explain the resonances
echoes & exceptions

the mother of God
in us   the mothers of sons
who had to be killed
& God in the mothers
whose sons had to be killed

Day 77

We tried to sing but ended up croaking
we who used to be songbirds

in time our throats had gotten dry

this is what happens when you start counting
days in hundreds from a date that never was

Another angle would have you believing
that this is how it went down
this & specifically this
they will be right

this is how it went down
there were days upon days
days upon days
days upon days
days upon days
that never seemed to end

who's to say when the first of a hundred days began

Day 75

There is evidence
that this was a conspiracy of silence

the insistence of green grass
the luminosity of a full moon
the leathered skin of the dead
the smile of skulls
flowers
the roar of the rushing river
the endless endless hills

if there was a shocked response
if this was an unnatural state of being
if this was a never ever situation
why didn't the world turn upside down

In thirty-nine days
there will be no more hindsight for sure
today already there's hardly any
no foresight
no insight
no encryption
no rules
no code

in thirty-nine days like today
there will be the same dullness about
the same powdery taste to everything
the same floaty feeling
the eerie pull to something beyond now

ants keep busy
they have figured out that life is for living
& death is for dying

there is no space for those of us
who are not dead
& have yet to be resurrected

Day 73

There are witness stones along all roads

between Jinja & Kampala
the road to Damascus
the roads leading to Kigali or Rome

there are stone witnesses
even on the road less travelled

stones witness along
the old majesty of Kenyatta Avenue
Khao San, Via Dolorosa
& the Sea to Sky Highway
where every few steps they say
is marked by the blood
of a foreign & indentured worker

did you know stones to scream

they did in those days
& they still do sometimes

The difference between the top screw
& the bottom screw is direction

we are squeezed in by past & present
& everything
everything is relative they say
god & religion
escape
in the name of forgiveness
reconciliation
& clean heartedness

be like Jesus   forgive
be like Jesus   remember to pray
& to pay taxes
be like Jesus   wear robes
have your first cousin shout in the streets
about the second coming of yourself
be like Jesus
hang out with prostitutes
love the sinner & all that

above all be like Jesus
demand an answer in the moment of your cross
to avoid the screw altogether

why God   why
have you forsaken us

Day 71

Who says alas in the presence of betrayal

who dizzies away
with swirling skirts & claims of nausea
alas alas all the hand-wringing

it shouldn't have been this way
it shouldn't

it shouldn't have been
forms the dregs from the past

would it have been better
that all this was lobbed at your head

would it have been better
if yours was the stuff of our nightmares

We became other people
we were them
those ones
who in being slaughtered & reported as slaughtered
lost any claim to intimacy or self

even animals don't commit slaughter

Day 69

The world turns as it does
spinning on its own axis
& then around the sun
& back & around

perhaps this galaxy
is also spinning around something bigger
perhaps all the worlds spin
to avoid dealing with the numbers

fourteen
three
all of them

six from my in-laws
& all of my siblings
his parents & their children

twenty-seven
thirteen
everyone
everyone
all of them
six
nine
twelve

my husband & all my children
all seven of them

two
nineteen
I don't know
I can't count anymore

nobody came back
I don't know if they ran away to safety
I don't know if they're rotating around the sun

I don't know if they're just all gone

Day 68

There's no denying that these haunted days
are not necessarily days of grey
there are flowers everywhere
beauty is always undeniable
these hundred days are haunted days not grey ones
these hundred days are filled with ghosted moments
just like every other day

Some days
I want to stare at the sky
perhaps I can learn something

some days
I think about how important the sky has become
I think about it & in so doing
I make it exist
I make the sky
an endless & expansive backdrop of blue

if there was a sky
how could it witness what it did
& still maintain that calm hue

could relate to how
the other areas of the
world moved on
and how other people
will never be able to
move on

Day 66

He was young
he was shiny
he was slim
he was brand

he was earth
he was sky
he was tremor
he was fall

he was chartered
he was bus
he was hampered
he was slowed

he was kind
he was vain
he was branded
he was armed

he was questioned
he was game
he was knowledge
he was stained

he was awed
keening
blurred
bloody serious
damned

Often times I want to become words
I want to inhabit forgetting as a state of being

sometimes I want to melt into the earth
I want to imagine that some time in the future
children will run over the soil that I've become

other times I think that if we wore a cloak of silence
our inaudibility would not be seen as invisibility
& our invisibility would not be seen as repair
or a sign that everything was good

the problem with becoming silence is that silence doesn't exist

it was never completely silent
nothing stopped to pay attention
nature chattered on
busy with life cycling
& subsumed us into the process

Day 64

There have been three so far
three men who walk with your gait
who turn   head first   the way you used to
walk like you did (sauntering like a cat)
laugh with your laugh
flick the wrist to make a point
the way you used to

three men who wore your face
for a moment lighted mine up

& then you were gone again
& they were just ordinary men
doing ordinary things

imposters
reminding me
that you used to be by me

Walter says life is hard
Walter says there is nothing we can do about it
Walter says I have to be happy to be alive

Walter says to be alive is better than being dead
be happy
Walter says
to be happy is to be alive

Day 62

Unless you believe in the eye of the needle
this kind of poverty will never be about material

it won't be about ragged clothing
or mud huts with broken walls
or river blindness
or murram roads
or bad-humoured fields that hoard curses
& promises that there won't be a harvest
this year or next year or ever

this isn't the poverty of sleep
or for that matter dreams

this is my deep loss
my poverty

he will never touch my hand again
he will never touch my hand

Incredulity is a soft-paced wonder
& in the thick of days
memory is a slippery thing   *repression?*

what do we remember from those one hundred days
what happened on the tenth day or night
might well have happened today or yesterday

incredulous is a naïve word
tepid & blubbery

because everything can happen
& everything did

Day 60

There used to be a joyousness in watching fish in water
gliding jumping
out & back in
out & back in
look   silver
look   black
look   red
look   grey
the river as a happy home to life

now globs of flesh
now pink spray
now whole bodies racing fish

look
the river   glad as a cemetery
the river   a happy home to death

So I must talk about what happened
talk that you may understand

because you want to understand
because you say
you want to make a difference
because all of it
begins with my telling of it

you want me to talk about what happened
you want me to tell
what was never mine to tell

Day 58

That we want
that we expect
that we earn what we get
that we want

that you don't
get

think again
think again

as long as we're caught
in the *neveragainness* of things
we are blinded
to the *hundreddaysness* of then

Day 57

We were halfway to dead when we were reminded
that we were halfway to dead

we were hovering suspecting tripping
or tiptoeing over the terrain
lest any semblance of confidence betrayed us again

ghosts flitted about
attentive to our progress
Chrissie knew
Chrissie could see
having never left ourselves
we were never going to arrive

Day 56

Before the maiden voyage
we heard that every water-faring vessel
needed sacrifice

the sacrifice had to be young
the sacrifice had to be blemish-free
the sacrifice had to have no dimples
no piercing in the ear
the sacrifice could be male
the sacrifice could be female

stay close to home
we were beseeched
stay close to home
lest the sacrifice-gatherers come by

we stayed close to home in those first days
we stayed close to home
but the sacrifice-gatherers didn't care for detail
they came to harvest bodies of all kinds
for a ship whose size has never been seen

There were no guards at the door
there was no door
& the only tax required was a last exhalation

our lives became both
endless & immediate

one moment you were alive
& the next gone

one moment
we were afraid of being heard
& then we weren't

one minute you were alive
& moments after that you wouldn't die
your chest gargled endlessly

one minute we cared
& the next nothing mattered

Day 54

It is absurd to think that a little girl will forget
how her mother's hands felt
when she used to plait her hair
some tugging
some lining on the scalp
with an oiled wooden comb
some cool oil
some warmth
when her hands gently repositioned her head
like so
sometimes a last pat on the back of her head
sometimes her neck

Okay, it's done, you can go out & play now

absurd that any little girl would forget that
& has

There were echoes if one listened for them
this wasn't the first time

there were echoes in Acholi
there were echoes in Armenia
in the Americas
Bangladesh
Bosnia
Cambodia
China
& the Congo
there were echoes in Darfur
there were echoes in England
there were echoes in Finland
in Georgia
Germany
Hawai'i
India
Ireland
Japan
Kenya
Latvia
& Mongolia
there were echoes in Nairobi
& echoes in Orange County
& Ovamboland
Poland
Palestine
Queensland
Russia
& South Africa

Southern Sudan
Tonga
Uganda
Vietnam
Wales
there were echoes in
xenophobic attacks everywhere
Yugoslavia
Zimbabwe

the earth palpitates as if it needs violence
as if violence is a heartbeat
if not here   over there
if it's not over there
it's on its way over here

ours wasn't the first or the only one
it was merely our most painful

So what if we were all Christian

would the media brand it
Christian-on-Christian violence

how do the dead declare
the part of their identity they were killed for

Day 51

I waited for my heart to harden
after the children were gone

I waited for the years of love to dissolve
as if they never happened

I waited for the day
when the remembrance of silly family laughter
would disappear with the setting sun
& I would wake up innocent
as if I had never known anything good

it was starting to happen in small ways
I couldn't recall the last good day

& then all the flowers bloomed
at commemoration
wreaths & ribbons & bouquets
thousands & thousands & thousands of flowers
each dead at the stalk
all dead from the moment they were cut
every single one dead
in their glorious & beautiful selves

just like the children
in those one hundred days

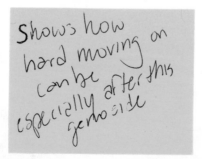
Shows how
hard moving on
can be after this
especially after this
genocide

This is the nature of our haunting
silent witnesses & silence itself
neither revealing nor capable
of explication

what do we need nature for

all it does is replicate its own beauty

Day 49

There we were
lining up like frauds
receiving medals & commendations
like frauds

there we were
listening to speeches
& reading adorations
about us as heroes
like frauds
holding in ourselves
like frauds

when all we did was stay alive
while many many others died

guilt for
being alive?
or anger for being
congratulated for
being alive when
they tried so
hard to save
others?

Day 48

What is it to be alive today

I no longer think about the hard beneath my feet
or the give of my body into sleep
or the way my skin used to dissolve
so deliciously from your touch

is this what it is to become a haunt

Day 47

My sister used to look up
when she remembered

sometimes she would have a small laugh
before she started to recall a story

often she'd be laughing
at the reverie & then we'd all start to laugh

& soon enough we were all laughing so hard
because she was laughing

& then she laughed because we laughed
& the memory of that story
dissolved into laughter & became infused with it

my sister is not here
I wonder if she remembers laughing
I wonder if she remembers anything

If truth is to be known
or acknowledged
then this is the truth that we know

we know the numbers
we know the number of days
we know the circumstances
where the machetes came from
& who wielded them
we know where the dotted line was signed

we know who fled
& who advanced
while chanting our names out loud
the names they called us
& the papers & airwaves
on which these names can still be found

we know who claim to be the winners
& the victims
we know where the markers are
for where we buried the children

we know
the impossibility of knowing everything that hap
we know that true witnesses cannot speak
& that those who have words
cannot articulate the inarticulable

we know that there are those who died
without telling what they knew
we know that there are those who live
without telling what they know

we also know that some people choose to tell
& some stories choose to remain untold

A lot is left
unsaid so
we will never fully
know everything
that happened

We watched as faith crumbled off the walls
in dull clumps

we watched as prayers dissipated into clouds
then watched them return as drizzle to mock us

sometimes it rained
sometimes it rained hard
sometimes it rained
as if the earth was sobbing
(but it was never so)
the earth remains dispassionate

eventually our superstitions burst like bubbles
or floated away like motes in the light

there was nothing left to hold on to
not even time which stretched
& then crunched itself wilfully

cats & dogs roamed about
feral & hungry
people crouched in the shadows
not all feral & all the time hungry

at a half past all time
even decay stopped for a moment

ours remains Eden
not even a spate of killing can change that

Day 44

Days & days of shallow breathing
interspersed with deep sighs
days zooming into nothing
days of years & years that morphed into decades
of life as a gift of life as worth living
days on days
days on days
we weren't even counting

it wasn't as if after all those days
a veil would lift
as if it would have taken just those days
& nothing more

it wasn't as if after all those days
there was a chance that normal
would be spat back out

as if all the seeds that had sprouted
in those one hundred days
would un-sprout themselves into nothingness

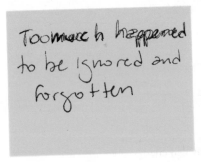

Too much happened
to be ignored and
forgotten

After all the madness
(& it had to have been a madness)
hear the arguments & explanations
that it was inevitable
that it was coming
that it had to happen after all those years

knowing what we know now
what else should we have expected

that my loss was inevitable
that my loss was coming
that my heartbreak was written in the stars
& in historical documents
& even in the oral tales

that we had to have been blind & deaf & dumb
to not have known
that we had to have been oblivious
to think that we could live
to a full life of family & community
like other people elsewhere

it was inevitable
we hear
but who fails to notice a genocide

Day 42

I kneel before you
but this is not an act of supplication
I kneel before you because I cannot stand
I kneel before you because I cannot speak right now

my gestures are wordless articulations
& the dark in my eyes is not an indication
of anything you could imagine
& there is nothing nothing that you could ever give me

If Justice was in a race against Time
Peace would have no medal to offer

if Peace sat at the table with Justice
Time wouldn't be served

if Time wanted Justice so bad so bad
there would be nothing that Peace could offer
either by seduction or reason

Day 40

She is my country

every time she goes
I am a leaf in the wind
every time she goes
she takes with her
all the home that I can ever claim

what use do I have
for the carrier of bones

what anthem can I sing
for the graves of children

she holds my home in the country that she is
& every time she returns
she is my flag & I am home again

If we were to go back
to the time before these hundred days
we couldn't return without knowing
what was to come

how could we

if we were to swear off
that we couldn't return to these days
I don't know that we could

we know
& we're marked by this knowing
we know

we know that we're marked
& this knowledge taints us

& so we know
that we can no longer absorb innocence

& innocence will not shield anyone from these days
& innocence does not cleanse
& innocence will not save us
from what we now know

Day 38

If there's a breeze tonight
we might think for a moment that i

there is a breeze tonight
& it is sweet

I can't remember if the breeze was sweet in those days
there was a breeze
it might have been sweet

it might have been
the same sweet breeze that kept us from burning

respite
-The Iliad
↓
Iris: "the respite in war
is brief"
(18,201)

When Christ lost a beloved friend he cried out
Lazarus!
Lazarus, come out of the tomb
Lazarus, come out of the tomb

imagine Christ crying for the beloved on this land
Lazarus! Lazarus! Lazarus! Lazarus!
Lazarus, come out of the tomb!

imagine Christ with a croaking voice
Lazarus, Lazarus, Lazarus!

Christ in a whisper
Christ mumbling
Lazarus, Lazarus

Christ spent
Christ crumbled
Oh, Lazarus

Christ either had no idea of these one hundred days
or he must have lost his voice in the first few moments

Christ may just have not been capable
he might have noted the endless & boundless
losses of the beloved on this land

Christ might have hung his head
completely powerless

> *questioning faith & the presence of God and Jesus*

Christ
look to your mother
ask her to pray for your intercession

Oh I curse you
I curse you long & hard & deep & wide
I curse you with fire from my mouth
I join everyone with fire in the mouth
wherever we live & wherever we lie
we curse you
we curse you
we curse you

Day 35

There's no denying the flap of an angel's wings
for someone who felt it fan her face in those days

the salve of a gentle touch
the stretch of an arm to catch you
as you reached for the top of the wall
the strength of a wail
the depth of a moan
the light of unending days
the consistency of seasons
as real as angel wings

there is a slope that leads
from these days of fiction
into nightmares that are real

So we saw & tasted & smelled & touched
felt & heard what we knew to be true

we had to see & taste & smell & touch & feel & hear
in order to know genocide

would one less death have disqualified those hundred days
from being called a genocide

& more
how it is the intention of others
& their numbers
(not our lives   not our losses)
to define genocide

One number or one death should not change what happened, the "genocide" classification shouldn't mitigate what happened

Day 33

So we mothed along towards the fire
with the full knowledge
that there couldn't be anything else beyond this

we mothed along
with bare arms wingless

a light step here
a light step there
sometimes no step at all
& other times dreamless stops

we mothed along knowing that it was possibly death
& not fire that beckoned

In Eden
we heard birdsong & didn't hear it
we saw the soft flutter & sail of a falling leaf
but we didn't know how to read it
we worked the earth   lived off it
trampled it back & forth
back & forth

in Eden
we never thought
about the difference between house & home
we never even thought to call it
we were it   it was us & ours
gaŋ wa

now as we fall unendingly
we know different
we understand belonging as transitory at best
& as elusive as the future we once imagined

Day 31

It is daytime now
we're here
it is now twenty years
after a hundred days
that we did not plan on living through

we wanted to prayed yearned to make it
not that those who didn't didn't

everyone prayed
to make it
through

A grid
a fence
a field
some grass
some stumbling

a ditch
mud
a broken slipper

a tear
a sheet
a groan

a metal plate with a faded rose
a rusty kettle that will never boil

Day 29

Time is a curve
so long that it seems to be a straight line

I can see myself walk away
I see & then remember
my heel striking the ground first
the weight of my shoulders
the back of my head
& the low hang of my neck

circle forward
what does my face matter if my heel is still cracked

When I (survey) look out at the world around me
(the wondrous cross)
on which (the Prince of Glory) every one that I loved, died
(my richest gain) My richest gain?
my richest gain?
I count (but) as loss
it was all loss all of it
& so I pour contempt on all (my) the pride
that seems to think that there is anything to celebrate

don't ever forbid it Lord
that I should (boast) dare to speak out
(save in) on the deaths
(of) Christ my God everything
everything that mattered
all the vain things that charm (me) you most
the sky scrapers
the clean streets
& the moneyed vendors

(I) You sacrifice (them) your own morality (to his blood)

there is nothing to party about
nothing

see from (His head His hands His feet) this vantage point
just how much sorrow
& love & bone & blood flow mingling down
did e'er such love and sorrow meet?
did ever?

where did ever such a twisted sense
of wreath making come from?
or why would thorns compose so rich a crown?
Christ
can you not read the land?

were the whole realm of nature mine
that were a present far too small
love so amazing so divine
demands my soul   my life   my all
so it took my soul my life my all

Glory be to the Father to whom all this is his will
glory be to the Son
who claims to have died for the sins of all men

glory be to the Holy Spirit
that guides the tongues of flames of the believers
as it was in the beginning
as it was in the beginning
as it has always been

as long as we need to hark back to a beginning
that only exists in the memory of the elusive trinity
who can only be accessed through faith
nothing will ever change
nothing will ever change except by faith
so nothing will change

Day 26

That day dared to set
as did the one after it & the one after that
days became long nights
that became mornings that appeared innocent
of the activities of the day before

that day shouldn't have set
the next day
if that other day had collapsed from exhaustion
should have held the night sky at bay

that day should have remained fixed in perpetuity
so that we would always know it to be real & true

Bones lie
bones lie about their numbers & bits & parts

bones lie in open air
in fields   under brushes
along with others in state vaults
in museums as if they belong there
in piles   as if they would ever do that in life

bones lie about being dead
bleached
broken
pulverized as if we who are not all bone
don't live with nightmares

bones have nothing to say
nothing about who it was that loved them the most

Day 24

& then there was just the two of us
everything in flames

the two of us
your arm around my shoulder
mine around your waist
we hobbled on
just the two of us

we hobbled on
for a while
& then there was just me

how hard it is
to survive and
help others.

Day 23

Some of us fell between words
& some of us onto the sharp edges
at the end of sentences

& if we were not impaled
we're still falling through stories that don't make sense

Day 22

Twenty years later we're young again
as we should be
welcome to this country
welcome

come & see
how we live
how we get over everything
how we exhibit skulls
how we caress skeletons
& tell stories about who these bones were

come & see how easy we are with things
come visit

our country is now open for tourism

- the landscape
has moved on but
the people haven't

the tourists have
no clue

A ring around a rosy
a ring around a posy
a ring around a peony
a ring around a buttercup
a ring around a baby's breath
a ring around a bouquet

a pocket full of posers
a pocket full of diamonds
a pocket full of memory
a pocket full of justice
a pocket full of ideas
a pocket full of shit

ring around a rosy
a pocket full of posies
achoo! achoo!
we all fall down!

Day 20

It has been called a harvest of death
but it was more like a net that was cast
a fisher net
a fisher net cast by a man
a fisher of men

Christer was that you

So this is what the Greek storyteller foretold

first the pity-inducing event
those poor poor people
pity in the numbers
pity in the grotesque photos that followed
the writing & the reading that followed that

there was nothing
nothing we could have done different
everything was beyond us

then came the fear it would spread like contagion
uncontrolled like a forest fire

& now it is time for catharsis

Day 18

Yesterday tripped & fell into evening
as it plunged deep into the night
voices rose up from the abyss

come! come! they called
come!

we never slept
trying to make sense
of whose voice was whose

yesterday tripped & fell into a long night
of calling   of voices beckoning
recalling things done
& things undone by time

today I'm busy
I'm trying to sort out the differences
whose voice was whose
which place what time

they all sound the same now
the dead & the unborn
they all sound quite similar

One day we woke up
& saw that we had all grown enormous horns

we took up enormous space when we moved
so that our horns didn't clash

each of our mouths was stuffed with a whole orange
we couldn't speak

another day
we woke up
with the hoofed feet & hands that you see on us

clop clop
clop clop
clop clop

still alive
still life

Day 16

Days & nights worked in tandem
to make us forget
that we were the carriers of events

we carried proof of place
& proof of time
we recited these details
over & over
we marked our steps
we marked the cadences into a rhythm
& held them close to heart

The 100 days
will always live
on through those
who experienced it
and those who will
tell the stories.

& so I am now a slow burning woman
creeping through time like a gecko through a tree
I'm shedding skin then eating it up
shedding skin then eating it as I crawl along

height like time has a hazing effect
but wonder remains
exclusive to the uninitiated

trying to move
on but there will
always be
reminders

Day 14

Now their eyes
flit flit flit
flit flit flit
like dragonflies in the afternoon
their hands are calm as they write
but clammy in the handshake

what can we do for you
what can we do for you

their eyes like dragonflies
what can they do for you

There was a rainbow in that sky
the day a chain-link fence separated us
on this side, we mixed nightmares with legend
I don't know what you did on the other side

you probably saw the rainbow in the sky
the chain-link fence
you probably saw it as well

people experienced
different things
even if only
seperated by a
fence but sharing
the same rainbow

Day 12

What now

now we must create our own world
use the right words
for the world we want to live in
like God

let there be light
& there was light

let us forgive our enemies
let us be good examples for the next generation
let us belong to one another
let us be friends

Day 11

Savage savage savage
savagesavagesavage
sa vedge sa vedge
sav edge sav edge
save edge save edge
saved saved
saved

Day 10

Stuffed
hacked
punched
pumped full of bullets
slaughtered
& left to rot on the street

pigs
dogs
cockroaches

people murdered
calculated & rated on a per hour basis
& sometimes exacted to ethnic & tribal
differences
struggles
divisions
clashes

never people you know
until they are

> people being reduced to
> less than human.
> – numbers and numbers
>   taking the human out
>   of them
>
> – anyone could die, having
>   the same fate by chance
>   not choice.

Some days
circle & circle
some days soar above like kites
some days
like hyenas waiting for the story to die

some sit
some stand on long legs
vultures wait
some stay some change seats
others come & go
some dive in
some walk crawl cycle
dial on the radio
to listen
to stories in embers
stories aflame
stories in stories
stories stoking stories
stories stalking stories
stories in circles & circles

those stories haven't yet killed me

Day 8

This is the horror that did not turn you into stone
this is the poem   the mirror   with which you can behold
that you did not turn into stone
this is true
you're still not stone

> people gained
> strength from the
> 100 days? It
> didn't completely
> break them?

We stumbled into the river
where words go to die
& where words come from

first we bathed in it
then we washed ourselves
we rinsed our mouths out
shampooed our hair
swam in words

& at night
we covered ourselves in words
& went to sleep

at night
the nightmares returned
but the dreams also came

certain areas and
things will never be
rid of the memories
(eg: the river) some
things will never go
back to how they
were before

↓
the river will
never just be a
river again.

Day 6

Images from those days return like silent movies
the available light from the rest of this life
& I can see
but I can't hear
anything

just the whirr
of silent movies

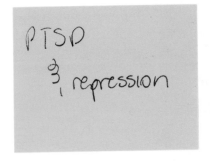

What do I remember
nothing but the contagion of stories
what do I want to say
what do I want to say

State of
shock, disappointment
and heartbreak .

Day 4

I have nothing

I stand before you with nothing
I am nothing

you stand before me with nothing

I don't know what I know
but I know that you know nothing
are nothing

I am nothing
& having come from nothing
to nothing & from nothing
let my nothing meet your nothing
& make nothing

} those with
nothing should
help each other
instead of
tearing each other
apart

We were pock-marked by
a torrent of accusations falling like rain
bayonet sticks
lies

we were mocked
by faith in tiny shards
by the cross with its pliant figure
representing grace
or representing the presence of God

what God in such a time
what God afterwards
what God ever

question of faith

- where was God
when they needed
him most?

Day 2

This will not be a litany of remembrances

we know who the guilty are
the guilty know themselves

this is a charge
against the witnesses
& those who cannot speak

against those who speak incompletely
& against those who speak incoherently

against nature who saw everything
& did nothing
against the bodies that dissolved
& the bones that refused to dissolve

this is a charge
against pain
against those who insisted
on writing the landscape with bones
against heartbreak
against laughter
against the dead

Acel aryo adek aŋwen
acel aryo adek aŋwen
acel aryo adek aŋwen
acel aryo adek aŋwen
acel aryo adek aŋwen
acel aryo adek aŋwen

we have run out of days

Author's Note

AT THE BEGINNING OF APRIL 2014, Wangechi Mutu,
a Kenyan American artist, posted daily photographs tagged
#Kwibuka20#100Days on Facebook and Twitter. I knew imme-
diately that they presented an opportunity for me to engage with
the 1994 Rwanda Genocide, a period that I've thought about for
the last twenty years. I contacted her and we began a collabora-
tion of sorts; I wrote a poem and she posted a photograph for
all the hundred days that has come to symbolize the worst days
of the genocide in Rwanda. One hundred days of killing, one
hundred days of witnessing, one hundred days of everything
else that seemed to matter and then it didn't, it couldn't. And
just like that, twenty years had passed and there was a need to
remember.

In July 2008, I had attended the International Poetry Festival
in Medellín, Colombia where I met Yolande Mukagasana, a poet
from Rwanda who had lived through the genocide and had lost
her family in it. She spoke tirelessly about what it meant to have
survived those hundred days. Hers wasn't a litany of losses, and
yet she'd lost her whole family. She spoke from an incredible
place of strength and pain and received a tremendous applause
when she delivered her poetry. I couldn't forget her and so when
I started to write *100 Days*, I was thinking about voices like hers,
imagining a country of poets like her. How and where do the
experiences of survivors of genocide in Rwanda match those of
survivors from Bosnia and northern Uganda? All three places
were steeped in war and violence at the same time. What is it to
be from a place where bloodshed of your kin darkens the soil,
makes the river run red and that's not newsworthy?

I wrote furiously. I wrote every day. Sometimes more than
a single poem emerged and sometimes just fragments showed

107

up. I wrote like someone possessed. Every day I posted a poem alongside Wangechi Mutu's photos on social media. Sometimes the match was incredible even though we worked independently from the east and west coast of North America, she in the US and I in Canada. She, an American Kenyan artist and me, a Canadian Ugandan poet—we both had something to express about a war that was close enough to our homelands that it could have been ours. We come from the same region, from countries that have deeply been affected by violence, from pre-independence struggles to dictatorships and in Kenya, the post election violence in 1997. How could it be that we could have nothing to say? How could it be that the only Africans to think about the genocide would be from Rwanda? And yet the genocide was ours, too; it was a crime against us, East Africans and Africans. It was a crime, as all of them are, against all humanity.

For some people, time twists memories, intensifying them in some places and loosening them in the details that don't seem to matter. What one day was like from another, how cold it was, whether or not there were flowers alongside a ditch on a long road—these dissolve for some and for others they are the markers of time and distance in those days.

Here are *100 Days* as I imagined them. Stylistically, I draw from various narrative traditions. From the Acholi oral tradition, I take on a strong and ever present narrator as well as the call-and-response style of storytelling. From the Christian liturgy and the lyrics of the Anglican Church, I claim a space from which to question an enduring faith, and from the American Spirituals, a place to challenge it. I drew on the spoken word and conventional poetry that disrupts the conventions, but these outward forms mean less than knowing that these poems speak to memories of those days, in solidarity and in fact. These are voices that resist the dominant narrative and imagine other ways to think about those terrible days through to today. At least one poem is directly inspired by Yolande Mukagasana's stories. I am grateful to Wangechi Mutu for parting the curtain enough to give me the courage to be part of this conversation. I am also grateful to the readers who responded so heartfully and sent encouragement along the way.

The memory of the 1994 Rwanda Genocide cannot be contained within borders. I hope that *100 Days* will open the conversation on how to think about war in general and about one of the most enduring and painful episodes of our lifetime.

Acknowledgements

MUCH APPRECIATION goes to the first readers, every day
of the 100 Days: Omer Aijazi, Chrissie Arnold, Erin Baines and
Wangechi Mutu. Readers on social media supported and shared
these poems, sending them off to a myriad of spaces beyond the
places they first landed on Twitter, Facebook and Instagram.
Thank you to Alexander Best from Zocalo Poets for seeing the
poems through to Day 1. Cecil Abrams, James Gifford and the
faculty at Fairleigh Dickinson University, thank you. Jasmine
Prashad for your enduring loveliness, thank you. The Liu
Institute for Global Issues for providing a space to work and
exhibit these poems, thank you. Afuwa Granger, Veda Roodal
Persad and Aerlyn Weissman, thank you for your friendship.
The women in WAN (Women's Advocacy Network, Gulu), thank
you for defining resilience in the presence of and after mass
violence. Pilar Riaño-Alcalá for introducing me to the politics
of remembering and forgetting, thank you. Ashok Mathur and
Ayumi Goto for enduring generosity, thank you. Kalina Lawino
Kojwang and Koju Kojwang for keeping me whole, thank you.
Jenkins Laloyo for holding my hand this far, thank you. My
family, from where I come and to whom I return, thank you.
The people of Rwanda, northern Uganda and Kenya for the
struggle to life and love beyond one hundred days, thank you.

Other Titles from The University of Alberta Press

Trying Again to Stop Time

Selected Poems

JALAL BARZANJI

SABAH A. SALIH, *Translator*

978-1-77212-043-1 | $19.95 paper

978-1-77212-072-1 | $15.99 EPUB

978-1-77212-073-8 | $15.99 Kindle

978-1-77212-074-5 | $15.99 PDF

148 pages | Foreword

Robert Kroetsch Series

Poetry | Canadian Literature

small things left behind

ELLA ZELTSERMAN

978-1-77212-002-8 | $19.95 paper

978-1-77212-012-7 | $15.99 EPUB

978-1-77212-013-4 | $15.99 Kindle

978-1-77212-014-1 | $15.99 PDF

128 pages

Robert Kroetsch Series

Poetry | Canadian Literature | Immigration

Massacre Street

PAUL ZITS

978-0-88864-675-0 | $19.95 paper

978-0-88864-819-8 | $15.99 PDF

128 pages

Robert Kroetsch Series

Poetry | Canadian Literature | Historiography